Lyrics of Life

in four-part harmony

Lyrics of Life

in four-part harmony

Larry Pontius

For my friend Joan
Larry Pontius
7/05

Aventine Press

Cover design and graphics by Jason Martin
http://www.conceptcreature.com

Published by Aventine Press
1023 4th Ave #204
San Diego CA, 92101
www.aventinepress.com

ISBN: 1-59330-297-5

Printed in the United States of America

For Harriet,
the love of my life
and my rock.

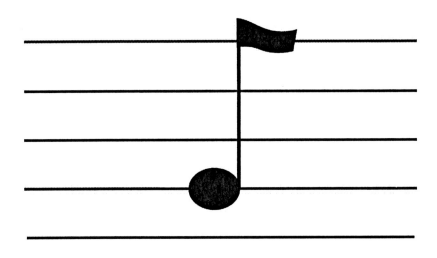

PART ONE

The poems for the book and spoken album *Warm Harbor and Other Places to Hide* were written as a 30th birthday present for my first wife, Catherine. It was created while we were living at a distance from much that we knew, during the years we lived in Australia. The book cover was designed by Grey Advertising Pty. Ltd. art director, Ray Harrington. The album was produced with the help of Charles Wolnizer at his Amalgamated Pictures Australasia studios at Kings Cross in Sydney.

Warm Harbor and Other Places to Hide

Warm Harbor

Maybe you wonder
What I do
After I kiss you goodbye
Every Morning
I've never told you
Have I

Oh, I know you think
You know what I do
I work
But just between you and me
That isn't exactly true

You see, I'm not a working man
At all
I'm a Captain
Of a paper boat called Life
And every morning
When I hear the screen door fall
I set sail
On a sea of lonely hours
Through a storm
Of trouble and strife

Wash the dishes
And I'm crashing through
A school of hungry fishes
Clean the floor
And I'm charting courses
Where even Cook hasn't been before
Darn a sock
And I'm battening down the hatches
To meet the waves
Of some little boy's rock

And later
With the smell of dinner
Cooking on the stove
I'm standing spread-legged
On the quarterdeck
Giving every oarsman
A roaring heave-ho

The storm is behind
The world isn't flat
The car lights bounce
From a white picket fence shine
And the Captain is over the side
Home again
To his Warm Harbor place to hide

Lancelots and Guiniveres

Every year they come again
Pug- nosed and pigtailed Guiniveres in distress
And awkward little Lancelots
Out to slay themselves a dragon
Wearing dress ups or tennis shoes and blue jeans
And riding little red wagons

Maybe you remember
The boy you used to be
And the time you said you'd be richer
Than J. Paul What's His Name
Me -- I was going to be Trigger
Except with a black mane

Funny actually
You know today I can't even whinny
But the kid next door who always wanted
To play Einstein came pretty close
He's balding in the right spots
And doing scientific tests
Just outside of Los Alamos

That's the trouble with being
Fledgling Lancelots and Guiniveres
It's so easy to grow up
And find all those dragons
You were going to slay
And all those black prince's dungeons
Where you and I used to play

Old Friends

Talking to someone
You've known for more than a year
Is a lot like talking to the face
In your bathroom mirror
That's the nice thing
About having old friends
You don't have to worry about
Conversations with two ends

Lovelock

Hardly anything makes a man feel better
Than twisting a key in the back door lock at night
Except maybe twisting another one in the front door
And leaving on the bathroom or hallway light

Not for himself, of course
Everyone knows grown men aren't afraid of the dark
I've seen even young men going for
Midnight walks in the park
On a dare

Now don't misunderstand
I mean what I say
There may be things in this world
To put fear in a man
But it takes more than just
The ending of the day

The reason men feel so good
Turning keys and lighting lights
Is because it makes their wives
And little ones feel safe
Protected from the dragons of the dark
By bolted doors and shining sleeping knights

And one more thing
Those turning keys and lighted hallways
Tell a man he's about to shut another kind of lock
The one that makes him feel safe
Protected from the dragons of the day

A Pocket Full of Dimes

Years ago
When I was living alone
I used to think the only way
I'd ever talk to anybody
Was by long distance
On some public phone

Sometimes I thought
I'd go out of my mind
Always worrying
Putting my hands in my pockets
Checking for a dime

And you know how that is
Every time you close yourself up in a phone booth
Someone fills you pockets up with bills

But like I said
That was long ago
Since then I've put a wife
And two kids in my home
And found out what it is
That makes a man feel so alone

It's not just being by yourself, you know
It's the fear of having to stay that way
For tomorrow and the next
And the next day

So maybe you understand
Why today phones are the last thing
On my mind
And why I call the wife and kids
My pocket full of dimes

You Can't Get There From Here

I don't know why
We struggle so hard
To get to Perfect
It's as easy
To get there as
Walking out in the backyard

All you have to do
Is turn left at Almost
Or is it Try
Well, anyway
I know once you make the turn
It's a down hill coast

Come to think of it
Maybe it's right
Instead of left
And maybe it's a block
Beyond Try
Do you know a street
Called Our Best

No – that's not it, either
There's no turn sign there
Not only that
The local council
Hasn't voted yet
To put that street on the map

I'll tell you what
You meet me some night
And I'll give you directions
But don't forget the beer
'Cause I got a funny feeling
You can't get there from here

Rain House

Sometimes I think
I'm living in someone else's house
When it starts to rain
I know darn well
This is where I've always lived
But somehow nothing seems the same

Maybe it's just the blowing wind
I hear knocking on the windows
That makes the rooms seem
So much warmer
And maybe it's that drooping gray
Just hanging there outside those windows
That makes the walls seem
So much whiter

Maybe it's just the sounding noise
Of someone out there throwing
Half the sea
That makes the house seem
So much quieter
And maybe it's the way
A rainy day looks so lonely
That makes the hours seem
So much happier

I don't know
But if I were a romantic
I just might tell a story
And this is how
It would go

Every time it rains
There's a marriage in the sky
Between a puff of wind
And a racing cloud on the fly

And the raindrops
We see here on earth
Are just the tears of a breath of air
Bride in mirth

And the reason
My house doesn't seem the same
Is because the groom and his spouse
Have chosen it for their honeymoon Rain House

Ten Cents Worth of Philosophy

There's not much you can do anymore
With just ten cents in your pocket
Last time I checked you could get
A Baby Ruth half the size they made before
And I hear you can still buy an hour
On some parking meters in Nantucket
But that's about the end of the line
In New York you can't even make
A phone call for a dime

I don't mind admitting
It's been worrying me for some time now
I've been wondering about what
We can find to do with this
fossil we call a dime

I guess that's how I came
To conjure up this ten cents worth
Of philosophy in rhyme:
It's a two sided coin we live
And for every heads we want to take
There's a tails we've got to give

On the other side of happy
There's a well that's full of tears
On the other side of courage
There's a mountain built of fears
And you can't know smiles unless you've cried
And you can't know brave unless you've died

On the other side of knowing
There's a dark and empty room
On the other side of growing
There's a season in the bloom
And you can't be smart before you're dumb
And you can't be old before you're young

On the other side of freedom
There's a cage of things to do
On the other side of wanting
There's a box of gifts from you
And you can't know free until you're tied
And you can't know have until you're tithed

It's a two sided coin we live
For every heads we want to take
There's a tails we've got to give
And it's no use trying to hide
'Cause a life can't come up heads
Unless there's another side

Tomorrow

I think we should
Change the spelling of tomorrow
To something a little sadder
Like pain or sorrow

It only makes sense
When you consider how much we pay
To make sure we reach
That land of borrow

We could buy yesterday
For just the price of a book
And today --
Well, all we have to do is
Open our eyes and look

But no --
We have to go right on robbing the past
And selling today for a one way ticket
To some fabled morrow
Only to learn when we get there
That it's today
Not tomorrow

Home

There must be a million songs
About being away from home
Now that I'm away myself
I suppose they should make me
Want to reach for a phone
But they don't

They give me a sad all right
But not the kind that makes
you think of phones
The kind you get when
you think of the men
That wrote those songs
Who never had a home

The Second Million Times

How do you say I love you
The second million times
After you've used up
All the special looks
Unexpected flowers
And quotes from favorite books

I can't think of any more
places to walk alone together
That we haven't walked along before
And the only way I can surprise you
With a visit on the phone
Is to call someday
When I know you're not at home

There isn't another place
On your soft skin
That I can give a loving touch
We covered all of that long ago
When our lips learned
Every loving kiss
And our passions
Every loving way to go

Is it possible
That love only has
A million signs
I guess that's what
I'm trying to say
That – and how'd you like
To start over
Like we just met yesterday

Keeping Secrets

There's nothing I love more
Than having a secret
And nothing I hate more
Than having to keep one

I can keep a secret
secret from anybody anywhere
As long as they don't care
But a secret isn't really a secret is it
When no knows it's there

So I hint and hedge
and laugh about the edge
Until it isn't anymore
And to tell the truth
I don't feel worse, I feel better
Than I did before

Because the magic in a secret
Isn't keeping it from those
For whom you care
It's the joy in telling it
For the two of you to share

The Boob Tube

Television
It's a modern miracle
At least that's what the television people say
And I guess it must be
How else could you get
200,000,000 minds joined together
To watch almost as many dots
Talk about the weather

And who would have believed
Ed Sullivan, Matt Dillon
And Mickey Mouse
Would someday push Mozart
Hemingway, Beethoven
And Shakespeare
Out of the house

Why I even hear
We can thank TV
For giving marriage new hope
People only talk during the commercials
And who can have an argument
In the time it takes to sell a bar of soap

But with all these miracles
There's still one thing I just don't get
How come my TV keeps playing the same old movie
With some purple-eyed, six-legged alien
Who decides to take himself to our leader
And then walks up to a television set

How Far Away Is Far Away

How far away is far away
Is all the way over on the couch far enough
As far as a Boeing can fly in a day
Or is that just around the corner

I guess it depends
On what it is that's far away
Some of the closest things in my life
Are twelve thousand miles from
The nearest runway end
And some of the longest trips
I've ever taken were from the couch
To you in that old bentwood rocking chair

People say that distance
Makes the heart grow fonder
And I don't doubt it
But I know this too
Sometimes the fondness of the heart
Makes the distance grow longer

So if you ever get to feeling
I'm waiting for a Boeing to get me
Off the couch and over to you
Just remember it's my heart
That makes me seem so far away

The Cages In My Mind

When you're a man
How do you tell somebody you're afraid
You can say you're nervous or worried
In a pinch you can even turn a little pale
But you can't tell the truth

When you're a man
You have to find another way
To say what's on your mind
Because somewhere along the line
We got a couple of words mixed up

We can't blame Webster
His brand of courage says nothing
About being afraid
Just the mind, the spirit and the temper
That enables one to meet danger

But then, I shouldn't blame
anyone anymore
I've found my answer
It's not as easy as just saying you're afraid
But it's not that hard either

I took some imagination and a little wood
And whatever bars I could find
And now instead of saying I'm afraid
I spend my time putting another something
Into one of the cages in my mind

The Eternal Summer

Like everyone else
I spend hours and hours dreaming
of the eternal summer
Walking through winter
Looking for some place to march to
Where a warming sun
Is the only drummer

But maybe a little unlike everyone else
I hope I'll never find it
Deep down I've got a feeling
We need the gutsy drummer of a stormy day
Why else is the sky always bluer
When it peeks through a gray

The Late Former Latter

How many chances
Does love have to die
In the average, ordinary
run of the mill day
Every time I think about it
I want to bundle mine up
And run away

It's one thing
Being willing to give love
There's joy in that
But quite another
When you face the pain
Of having to take it back

Nobody likes an Indian Giver
So what's the joy
In being the latter
If some day you end up
being the late former latter

How Long Have You Been Waiting

Wait
Sometimes I think that's all
We ever do
It doesn't make any difference
Who you are
Even George Bush had to wait
For the vote to come through

I guess it starts
The first time we look up
From our crib
And realize that soft warm
One course restaurant isn't there
And it seems
It goes on until the day
We draw our last breath of air

How long have you been waiting
Let's see...
There was the day
You'd get to go to big kid's school
The genuine Dick Tracy super secret code book
The postman was bringing
And what ever happened the year
You asked Santa Claus for a swimming pool

I remember
The Monday I had the good luck to find
The paper hats for my own surprise birthday party
There should have been fifteen candles
On that Friday cake
Even though I was only nine

But I'll tell you what
We really don't have much reason to complain
You and I
When you think about it
Playing the waiting game isn't such a bad way
To pass the time of day
When you're also waiting
To die

The Cost of Growing Up

I never wonder
What happened to the child
I used to be
He simply grew up
And became the man I call me

But what happened
To all the butterflies he used to chase
And all the grassy hills
That used to scratch his back
While he watched elephants and tigers
Float across the sky
In a cotton candy race

What happened
To all those warm winter days
And all those double feature cowboys
Who rode across the popcorn dark
From noon to four on Saturdays

What happened
To all those Tarzans
Who had to promise his mother
They wouldn't get grass stains on his jeans
And all those white sheet ghosts and goblins
Who ate all that candy
On the day after Halloween

Did they grow up, too
Or did they die
All those elephants
And goblins and butterflies
I know I wanted to be
A grown man someday
But it still seems like a terrible price
For a little boy to pay

Man and Wife

What's the difference
Between man and woman
And man and wife?
Nothing, I guess
Except a life

A Last Cigarette

One of these days I'm going to fall
On these stairs in the dark
Where's the lighter and the cigarettes
Now find a place to park

"Why in the world do you
Have to smoke at midnight?"
This last cigarette wouldn't be complete
Without your question
Excuse me, while I give myself a light

Coffin nails and lighter fluid
Why does a man come groping
Downstairs at night to seek out his dying
Could it be he knows things aren't right
And smoking a cigarette is also a little like crying

The Lemonade Tree

Have you ever found a miracle
Growing in your backyard
I did yesterday
It seems my daughter planted it
Just by wishing hard
For a game to play

I know this sounds ridiculous
To adults like you and me
But for one moment
When she said, "Daddy look,
A Lemonade Tree!"
I thought I saw it

I thought I could feel the coolness
Of a leafy sweet shade
Hiding the sun
I thought I could taste
The sour of lemons
And the sugar of fun

Of course, you and I know better
There's no way to grow
A Lemonade Tree
What I saw and felt and tasted
Was a child's mind aglow,
The joy of being three

But still, there was a miracle
In my yard yesterday
No Lemonade Tree
But a miracle just the same
For a child at play
Touched the child in me

Yesterday, Today, Tomorrow

There's always something
To remember from yesterday
Or to look forward to tomorrow
That makes today seem a little pale

I remember the first girl I ever kissed
Now, that was a girl!
And if I ever told you about
The opportunities I've missed
Well – it would make your hair curl

But that's nothing
You ought to see the deal
I'm going to sign next week
And wait until I tell you about the club
That may ask me to speak

Poppycock?
Yes
But is it really such a sin
There's comfort in remembering
A past that never was
And a joy in waiting for
A future that will never be
I wonder what happens to
The today that could have been

Sleep

When I was young
And the night was forever
I used to wonder why
Older people liked to go to bed
Then suddenly the night was a woman
And I asked myself why the question
Ever entered my head

But now I'm not so sure
Maybe there's something more to say
About age and the troubled waters of the day
And an appointment we want to keep
With a black faced oarsman
In a lifeboat called sleep

When I Look Back From Tomorrow

What will I see
When I look back from tomorrow
What will we be
When we have no cloak to borrow

Madmen, Godmen
Heroes or Neros
Saints who died
Or just men who tried

Will we recall
A human footstep on the moon
A baby's mouth and golden spoon
Or a human bomb's burning bloom
A mother's babe with cast of doom

What will I see
When I look back from tomorrow
What will we be
When we have no cloak to borrow

Sinners, saviors
Lepers or Shepherds
Frails who cried
Or just men who tried

Will we re-live
The shinning moment peace came home
The dying desert turned to loam
Or the final end to man's lust
The richest earth turned to gray dust

What will I see
When I look back from tomorrow
What will we be
When we have no cloak to borrow

Doers, Dreamers
Pirates or Patriots
Gods who lied
Or just men who tried

Will we review
The dawning of the end of war
The sunrise that can come to poor
Or a billion lives spent for naught
A tragic play with mankind bought

What will I see
When I look back from tomorrow
What will we be
When we have no cloak to borrow

This Hurricane Called Life

Who hasn't felt the icy blast
Who hasn't heard the howling wind
Who hasn't seen the frozen breath
Who hasn't touched the driven rain
Of this hurricane called life

And who hasn't tried to find
A place to hide
Somewhere on this earth
Or in their mind

In Care Of Satan

Let's chase hate out from where it's hiding
Let's find a bait to make it come
Let's put it in a box with writing
And mail it back where it came from

Let's hunt the woods of our minds for fear
Let's set a trap and when it's been sprung
Let's wrap it up in a cardboard crate
And mail it back where it came from

Let's loose the hounds and make war the fox
Let's build a cage and when the chase is done
Let's tie it up with steel chains and locks
And mail it back where it came from

I can see a billion boxes
Stuffed all full of fear and war and hatin'
A billion better days in the makin'
I can see a billion boxes for the postman waitin'
A billion boxes marked "In Care of Satan"

The Heart Of A Child

In a world so full of hate and woe
With all Four Horsemen running wild
When I hear the ragin' fear wind blow
Lord, Lord, Lord
Give me the heart of a child

I gotta love my neighbor
Even when he's black or poor
I gotta give my money
But I don't know what for
I gotta taste the honey
And then march me off to war

I gotta find me a heart
For all that and much more
And the only heart with room enough
Lord, Lord, Lord
Lord is the heart of a child

In a time so gray there ain't no sun
With all them missiles being piled
When I feel that rippin' fear tide run
Lord, Lord, Lord
Give me the heart of a child

I gotta face friends and fight
Even when they're rich or white
I gotta live my own answer
But never know if I'm right
I gotta grow me a cancer
And die alone in fright

I gotta find me a heart
That can stand to cry all night
And the only heart with tears enough
Lord, Lord, Lord
Lord is the heart of a child

And my old heart ain't man enough
Lord, Lord, Lord
Give me the heart of a child

They

Why don't they turn the kickin'
soul-fightin' kept down black man free
Why don't they
Why don't they make the stinkin'
eye burnin' hot air over L.A.
clear enough to see
Why don't they

Why don't they give the dyin'
sick lyin' poor down and out
cash enough to buy a six by six
place to die
Why don't they
Why don't they face up,
wake up, shape up, grow up, own up
before the whole damned world gets blown up

Why don't they stop this dirty
boy bloodied endless war
Why don't they
Why don't they end the icy
hate breedin' stare that looks out
from each and every shore
Why don't they

Why don't they quit the lyin'
sick cryin' hypocrisy that makes us all
money grubbing two bit whores
Why don't they
Why don't they face up,
wake up, shape up, grow up, own up
before the whole damned world gets blown up

Why don't they breathe the air
down in your lungs
Why don't they
Why don't they hear the songs
you've never sung
Why don't they
Why don't they feel the stone
in your shoe
Why don't they
No, they can't face up,
won't wake up, can't shape up
won't grow up, can't own up
because there is no they
only you

PART TWO

In 1971 I was asked to help with the celebration in Australia of the 25th Anniversary of U.N.I.C.E.F. The 90-minute television special and album *For the Love of Man* were written in collaboration with musician, Julian Lee. The creation and production of this project could not have been possible without support from many sources including, Grey Advertising, Pty, B.P. Australia Ltd, Amalgamated Pictures Australasia, United Sound Pty. Ltd, Air New Zealand, Channel 7 Network, and others. I would like to express my appreciation to them and the artists who recorded the songs in Sydney and Melbourne, Australia as well as Las Vegas and Hollywood. The artists who performed gratis in the TV special and on the album included Robert Goulet, Mel Torme, Lainie Kazan, Joe Williams, Glenn Yarbrough, Sue Raney, Rim D. Paul, Johnny Farnham, Talya Ferro, Neil Williams, Tommy Leonetti, Judy Stone, Arch McCurdy, and Jimmy Witherspoon. Actor Eddie Albert was kind enough to donate his time and talent as host of the television program.

For the Love of Man

I am Man

I am yesterday
And tomorrow
I am the giver of joy
And the deliverer of sorrow
I am the tears of God
And the warmth of his smile
I'm a child's first step
And life's last mile
I'm the wingless eagle
And the hawk who cannot see
I'm all that could have been
And all that still may be
I'm the link that is weak
And the chain that is strong
I'm the sound of silence
And the voice of a song
I'm the reaper of love
And the sower of hate
I am my own destiny
And the follower of fate
I'm a single raindrop
And the flood in the pool
I'm a shining genius
And a stumbling fool
I'm the constant cleansing tide
And a footprint in the sand

I am Man

The News No One Wants To Hear

Have you heard the news today
It sounds like love walking away
That's what people want to hear
At least that what the men who wrote it say

But I wonder
What can you learn from bad news
'Cept how to cry and where to find the blues

Someday, yes someday we're going to hear
The news that no one wants to hear
Someday some one day we're going to hear the news
The news that no one wants to hear

Yesterday they used to say no news is good news
But today I hear them say good news is no news
And I'm confused
You tell me who's being used

Someday, yes someday don't you fear it
Someday we're going to hear it
The news that no one wants to hear

For the Love of Man

Somewhere there's a river
Running deep and rolling wide
Somewhere there's a river
Of tears I've cried
For the love of Man

Roll on you river
For all the dreams grown old
Roll on for all the young desires turned cold
Roll on you river
Ten thousand miles across the land
Roll on and lay down my tears on your thirsty sands
For the love of Man

Roll on you river
For all the challenges unmet
For all the promises unkept
For all the fear unfaced
For all the trust misplaced
For all the hate turned loose
For all the love unused

Roll on you river
Ten thousand miles across the land
Roll on and lay down my tears on your thirsty sands
For the love of Man

Someday you'll find the sea
And pour out your salty tide
And someday I'll dry my eyes
Of tears I've cried
For the love of Man

So roll on you river
For all we hoped we'd see
Roll on for all the things that still may be
Roll on you river
Ten thousand miles across the land
Roll on and lay down my tears on your thirsty sands
For the love of Man

The Devil's Well

You know I'm getting tired
And feeling so sick
From drinking hopin' water
And I see that filling cup
Of feeling better
Sweet tasting hatin' water

But every time I start to drink
I hear someone sayin' think man, think
Where did it come from that sweet tastin' drink
The Devil's Well, straight up from Hell
Yeah, The Devil's Well

Yes, that drink you think
Tastes so sweet
Ah, let it keep
'Cause you know man is more than beast
And beast less than man
But who can tell, from The Devil's Well
Even gold can turn to sand

I know that bitter cup
Of feeling so bad
From drinking hopin' water
And I see that other cup
Of feeling so good
Sweet tasting hatin' water

But every time I raise the cup
I hear someone sayin' man, look up
Where was it drawn from that sweet tastin' cup
The Devil's Well, straight up from Hell
Yeah, The Devil's Well

So drink man drink
That bitter cup
Drink it up
'Cause you know man is more than beast
And beast is less than man
But the twain can meet, yes they can
And they will, yes they will
If hope dies in this land

All God's Crippled Children

You may think I'm wrong
May disagree with my song
But I've got a feeling they'll be singing it
Long after you've gone

Praise the Lord
Praise the Lord
For all God's crippled children

You may never see
You may burn me and my song
But I've got a feeling that the ashes
Will never be gone

Praise the Lord
Praise the Lord
For All God's crippled children

Praise the Lord
Praise the Lord
For the blind man who knows
The fright of being without sight
And still has the will to bring the world light

Praise the Lord
Praise the Lord
For the deaf boy who knows
The sounds of silence evermore
And still will not hear the bay of pity's hounds

Praise the Lord
Praise the Lord
For all God's crippled children

Praise the Lord
Praise the Lord
For all God's crippled children

For the child without legs
Who refuses to beg
For the girl without hands
Drawing pictures in the sand
For the boy who cannot talk
Who still insists that we walk
For the young who must die
No one ever sees cry

Praise the Lord
Praise the Lord
For all God's crippled children

Praise the Lord
Praise the Lord
For all God's crippled children

For in their hidden fear
And in our falling tears
I hear a song for you and me
I hear a song of what man can be

Oh yes,
Praise the Lord
Praise the Lord
For all God's crippled children

Praise the Lord
Praise the Lord
For all God's crippled children

Funny Face

Hello, Funny Face
You're a sad, sad case
Little Funny Face

Why did your mother scold
You're only two years old
With your pout upon the ground
You're a three foot teardrop
With a seven foot frown

But a tickle right here
And a whisper in your ear
And a wiggle, and a giggle
And the tears disappear

Yes, your pout's up off the ground
And a giggle's going round
And any minute now you'll be wearing
A frown that's upside down

Ohh, hello Funny Face
You're a glad, glad case
Little Funny Face

You never have been told
You're only two years old
But in your Funny Face way
You save time to cry
And still have time to play

The Long Long Dark

If the birds forget how to sing
Who cares
If church bells forget how to ring
Who cares
If puppies forget how to bark
Who cares
Who cares, who cares, who cares
In this long, long dark

If the trees forget how to grow
Who cares
If winter forgets how to snow
Who cares
If lovers forget how to park
Who cares
Who cares, who cares, who cares
In this long, long dark

It's been a long time coming
And it'll be a long time here
Gone is the need for running
And there's nothing left to fear
And the long, long dark is here

If God never made the light
Who cares
If Adam never gave his rib
Who cares
If Noah never build the arc
Who cares
Who cares, who cares, who cares
In the long, long dark

Hallelujah Noah Is Born Among Us Again

Nobody knows when the wind started blowin'
Nobody knows when the rain started fallin'
And nobody knows when the flood started risin'
Higher and higher and higher

Oh, feel the risin' water swirling around us
Higher and higher
Feel the deep dark coldness about to drown us
Don't cry mama, don't cry
Your child mama, gonna live not die

I don't know when the trees started fallin'
And I don't know when that sound started rappin'
But I know that I can hear a strong man callin'
This way you and you
This way two by two

Hallelujah, Noah's born among us again
Hallelujah, and we'll all float away from our sin
Hallelujah, Noah's born among us again
And we'll all float away from our sin

Yes, I know we will hear the wind stop blowin'
And I know we'll hear the rain stop fallin'
And I know we'll feel the flood stop risin'
Yes, I know
'Cause I can hear a strong man callin'
This way you and you
This way two by two

Hallelujah, Noah's born among us again
Hallelujah and we'll all float away from our sin
Hallelujah, Noah's born among us again
And we'll all float away from our sin

Don't Give Up On Us Now

They said it couldn't be done
And it was, yes it was done

See it standing there in the frozen moonlight
Forty days walk from Katmandu
To climb that Everest peak
Is something no man will ever do
And is was, yes it was done

So, don't give up on us now, brother
Don't give up on us now
No, don't give up on us now, brother
We'll work it out somehow
We'll work it out somehow

See the Pyramids and the Golden Gate
See the moon and the atom, too
To reach the impossible
Is something no man will ever do
And it was, yeah is was done

So, don't give up on us now, brother
Don't give up on us now
No, don't give up on us now, brother
We'll work it out somehow
We'll work it out somehow

See them hiding there in the failing sunlight
Ninety years of hurt to get through
To heal this bleeding earth
Is something no man will ever do
And it will, yes it will be done

So, don't give up on us now, brother
Don't give up on us now
No, don't give up on us now, brother
We'll work it out somehow
We'll work it out somehow

The Child Who Takes My Place

How long before I stumble and fall in this human race
And what will he be like, the child who takes my place
I hope he cares about the small things in life
The wildflowers, the snowflakes
And the look on children's faces that only Christmas makes

And what will he be like, the child who takes my place
I hope that somewhere in his heart he has the room
For the sad things, the glad things
That make you cry because you feel so good

And where will he stand, the child who stands where I stood
I hope he sees the day when all mankind are free
With head held high
But most of all I hope he has a son who never learns
Never learns to use a gun

Generation Bridge

Tell the young man we don't need his shovel
Tell his father we don't want that pick axe on his shoulder
We've dug it deep enough this muddy pit of trouble
And the diggin' days are over

Generation Bridge
We can build it, yes we can
You and I dad, yes we can
Hand in hand on the Generation Bridge

Tell the young man bring a hammer full of love
Tell his father cut a forest full of days when he was the son
We're climbing way up above this muddy pit of trouble
And the building days have begun

Generation Bridge
We can build it, yes we can
You and I dad, yes we can
Hand in hand on the Generation Bridge

Tell the young man a bridge is not a chain
Tell his father you can only hold a babe but you can
talk with a son
We're working out all the pain from this muddy pit of trouble
And our crying days are done

Generation Bridge
We can build it, yes we can
You and I dad, yes we can
Hand in hand on the Generation Bridge

Give a Little Love

Give a little love
To someone you just met today
Give a little love
To help chase hate away
We're all children of a greater child above
So, give a little love
Give a little love

Give a little love
To someone you don't know today
Give a little love
To help chase fear away
We've all got to live like fingers in a glove
So, give a little love
Give a little love

A single smile, a nod, a wink
That's all you've lost, that's all it cost
But in return just stop and think
For someone you are the sunshine melting the frost

So, give a little love
Like some innocent child at play
Give a little love
And you'll feel good today
We've all got to float together in this boat
So, give a little love
Give a little love

So, give a little love
Like some innocent child at play
Give a little love
And you'll feel good today
We've all got to float together in this boat
So, give a little love
Give a little love

The Street of Hope

Every year they come again
Pug-nosed and pigtailed Guiniveres in distress
And awkward little Lancelots out to slay themselves a dragon
Wearing dress-ups or tennis shoes and blue jeans
And riding little red wagons

Riding little red wagons
Down the Street of Hope
A street with so much to give
The street where all the children live
The Street of Hope
The Street of Hope

The street with so much to give
The Street of Hope

Awkward little Lancelots and tiny Guiniveres
The only hope we'll ever have
Though we wait a million years
Tomorrow's gift from every man and wife
These miniature cobblestones of life
On the Street of Hope
The Street of Hope

The street with so much to give
The street where all the children live
The Street of Hope

Look up, look up
The Street of Hope
The street with so much to give
Look up, look up
The street where all the children live
The Street of Hope

That's The Way It's Going To Be

Sunday chicken dinner at the world
A drumstick and a wishbone to pull a wish on
For every little half pint
Biscuits and gravy for everyone to swirl
And later on the veranda
A billion cups full of afternoon tea
You may laugh, but that's the way it's going to be
Yes, that's the way, that's the way it's going to be

Monday noon time sun walks at the world
And somewhere in the park old crazy Harry
Still standing on his soapbox
Giving the same old speech with the same old curl
Once there was a time and a place
Where someone was chained instead of free
You may laugh, but that's the way it's going to be
Yes, that's the way, that's the way it's going to be

Yes, that's the way it's going to be
That's the world I can see
And it's up to you and me
Yes, that's the way it's going to be

Tuesday evening meetings at the world
Miss Walker's slides again on how to keep peace
A second hundred decades
And the talk somehow turns to the old, old world
Days no one here can remember
When somewhere men lived without dignity
You may laugh, but that's the way it's going to be
Yes, that's the way, that's the way it's going to be

Wednesday morning breakfast at the world
You're sleepy eyes hiding behind the paper
And little change in the news
Wednesday or Thursday they're planning to unfurl
Flags for the country of mankind
And Friday they're filling Saturday's needs
You may laugh, but that's the way it's going to be
Yes, that's the way, that's the way it's going to be

Yes that's the way it's going to be
That's the world I can see
And it's up to you and me
Yes, that's the way it's going to be

And you may cry
And so do I
But that's the way it's going to be
Yes, that's the way, that's the way it's going to be

God Child

Are you reaching out in the darkness all alone
Reaching through the night for someone, somewhere
Who will take your hand in his own
Are you listening there in the darkness by the phone
Waiting for someone to say hello and all the trouble it
has flown

Reach out, yes, reach out
Reach out and touch me
Touch me and we can make the darkness light
Yes we can, hand in hand
For we are man
The God Child man

Reach out, yes reach out
Reach out and touch me
Touch me and we can make the trouble right
Yes we can, hand in hand
For we are man
The God Child man

The devil may think he's got us
But old Satan he forgot
Forgot who it was that made us, you and me
For we are man, yes we are
The God Child man

If you're sitting there in the darkness with your tears
Crying for something that will help you fight
all your frustrations and fears
Just reach out, reach out, yes reach out and touch me
Together we can make the trouble right
Yes we can, hand in hand,
For we are man
The God Child man

PART THREE

The book *Buttermilk Sundays* was written for my beautiful wife, Harriet, who taught me that there is a place called Jackson, Tennessee and something called love. It is an often smiling and sometimes bittersweet tapestry of our lives together so far, and includes our wedding vows, Christmas cards, birth announcements, Sunday morning inspirations, and not a few late night ruminations.

Buttermilk Sundays

Buttermilk Sundays

They came to us as crystal gifts,
those long yawning Sundays,
empty and waiting
for the spring wine of our lives.
And we poured ourselves into them
like children splashing
into summer swimming pools,
filling the day with laughter and loving
as rich and sweet as buttermilk.

Tennessee Girls

The Beach Boys are frauds.
Singing that same old song
for more than twenty years
and never admitting the truth:
they never played Memphis.

Hard Times

I never knew his name
Only his face
And those shrouded sad eyes
that always yearned
for some other place
But he was always there
just the same.

I never heard him sing
Only his talk
the voice sounding so used
that gravel throat
so right for the blues
Still we walked together
down a string.

I never held his head
Only his hand
a pale, dusty welcome
that somehow said
once here was a man
And I knew which of us
might be dead.

I never knew his name
Until you came
with your cookies and wine
And something else
you called the Good Times.

And I still don't know his name
Only that he went away
On a Tennessee train.

The Jackson Smiths

A friend said
you came from Jackson
and I believed it.

But no more than I believed
your name was Smith.

And not nearly as much
as I loved you.

Of Christmas Carols

Who can say
how much Dickens has helped them
drift through dying days,
the Tiny Tims
hiding within us all?

I know that sometimes
I still dream of dancing
like Gene Kelly.

Harriet

From earth and sky she came,
half dream, half roots;
the dust of floured fingers
on aprons with Italian names,
a quiet whispered linger
in the fall of Peter Pan boots

A woman's stubborn strength,
a child's simple smile,
wife and lover,
daughter and mother
Tomorrow's ever opening circle
Yesterday's constant closing lariat

Harriet

Beautiful Words

Of all the words
we will write in the years to come
And all the words
we have spoken since we were young
The two most beautiful words
in the mind of Man
are those which once a year say,
Yes we can:

Merry Christmas.

Of Shoes and Children

There was a young woman
who lived in Florida
who had no children
and nothing to deplorida

So she married a man
who came with a clan
and moved to California

Circles

Within a circle of friends
the circle of hope is drawn again
Within this circle of gold
the circle of faith once more is told

Within a circle of friends
the circle of love is traced again
Within this circle of gold
the circle of life once more is whole

Watching Words Walk Up The Wall

Your sheet tangled body
lies asleep now,
wombed around a pillow
from Tennessee.

And, alone, I chase smoke dreams
through the night,
watching words walk up the wall
and fall off the ceiling
onto yellow pads.

Shhhhh!

You keep climbing
those feathered hills
all the way to Chattanooga.
Remember, yellow is your favorite color
and words have walked for ages.

On This Day

*On this day
may you sing the old songs
in the kinship
of friends and clan.*

*On this day
may you taste the honey
in the giving
to Brother Man.*

*On this day
may you see forever
in the birthglow
of Bethlehem.*

Television Redux

*I understand
our morals are shot to hell.
But who can tell
what secrets pass
between woman and man?*

*Could the big turn on
in most bedrooms
have more to do with TV
than You and Me?*

Close Your Eyes

Close your eyes
and open up a dream
of green dappled meadows
and bare feet
and cool running streams.

Close your eyes
and drift down the night
on kites made of jasmine
and roses
and swans taking flight.

Close your eyes
and listen for the dawn
and whippoorwills yawning
through sunrise
with love songs to sing.

Close your eyes
and slip away to sleep.
Shhh!
Not a peep.
Tomorrow will keep.

Why is Christmas?

"Why is Christmas, Daddy" he asked
And I tried to explain.

With Mary and Joseph
and Wiseman and kings
With cradles and mangers
and angels who sing
I talked and I talked
And I tried to explain.

With bread loaves and fishes
and Scrooge and Morley,
O. Henry and Dickens
'til my brain felt sorely
I talked and I talked
And I tried to explain.

But, alas, I despaired;
the secret remained
I couldn't make Christmas
two year old plain
though I talked and I talked still I failed to explain.

Then on Christmas yawning
a small voice whispered
from some small someone's bed
knowing someone heard
And I understood
what I'd tried to explain.

"Happy Birthday, Jesus!" he said,
Two year old plain.

Newberry Summers

Like faces in the misty light
visitors from Rome
come sailing home in arks
full of Kermits and kangaroos,
drawing dreams of bubble gum and baseball
in the sleepy heads
we put to bed at night.

And, for a time,
the world is warm again,
as it has always been
in the soft embrace
of our Newberry summers.

If I Had It To Do Over

If I had it to do over
I would spend more time playing with puppies
And stomping through mud puddles
I would take more long, hot showers
And spend more midnights looking up at the sky
I'd worry less about what people think
And more about what they need
I would listen to more music
And write more songs
And most of all
I'd meet you sooner

Your Space or Mine?

Just in case you wonder,
I don't – mind, that is.

When you beg off,
wrapping yourself in that musk cocoon,
drifting down to the river
on a snow sled pulled by herds of mice,
I spend my time boxing kangaroos
and polishing 55 flivers.

Besides, tomorrow never comes later than nine.
Your space? Or mine?

BrantleyBridge

I finally figured out
where it is,
that castle in the air
we built to hold our dreams

Somewhere in the green hills
of Tennessee,
on a Warm Harbor
by the sea

The Gift Each Was Wanting

I knew a man who had nothing
and yet on Christmas Day
he gave the gift
each was wanting
to all who came his way.

To some he nodded,
to some he winked,
to some he simply smiled.
And as they passed
he made them think
there is a Christmas Child.

The Big Mickey

I know I did it badly
But I hope you'll forgave
After all, it's not only what I hadly
it's also what I gave.

Rebecca

All the beautiful sights I've ever seen
are faded photos from a long forgotten dream
now that I've seen her mother's smile
on that first November morning
when Rebecca came a-borning.

Short Distance

Mothers always exaggerate.
I suppose that's why
Ma Bell calls it Long.
She wouldn't, you know,
if she knew how close
I feel to you
afterwards.

A Right Jolly Old Elf

Every year they come again
asking who is really him.
Why we stammer and stutter,
our hearts all a-flutter,
I never really understand.

We should be glowing,
happy in their knowing
that the Right Jolly Old Elf
is you and myself
and the Christmas Spirit
in the millions of others
we call Man.

Mad Money

Sometimes I talk so old
you must think my brain wears
worn out slippers
and baggy pants and such.

But I don't mind much.

You see, those old dungarees
have a secret pocket
where I hide a million dollars
worth of memories.

And no matter where I go,
I can always dip inside
and find enough mad money
for a taxi ride
back to you.

The Long Trips

They worry me,
you know;
those long trips
I take all the time.

Off to some airport,
hang bag in hand,
with the smile
on your kiss-crushed lips
and the little wave
that says everything's just fine
riding along
in the back of my mind.

I never told you why,
did I?

It's not that you
might not be there
when I get back.

I might not get back.

At Sixteen

She was tresses of soft ash
hiding the smile of Madonna
She was the shape of woman
hiding the mind of a Mozart
She was the soul of Mankind
Searching for some long lost freedom

The Greater Miracle

As you reflect
on the miracle of this day
- a child who was born
and born again
nevermore to die
save a thought
for the greater miracle:
that he lived at all
and so do you and I.

Who Do you Love?

You try to laugh it off,
but it hurts a little too
when you ask her
who she loves
and she mentions everyone
but you.

I know.
I watch the way you walk
after those bedtime talks
And I also know
I wouldn't squawk.

How many two year olds
learn the names of
sister, friends and brothers
just to play a love game
with Mother?

I Never Wanted to be a Spaceman

I drank the wine Serling sipped
Ate a loaf of Bradbury bread
Walked the path where Asimov led
And felt the drive of Bova's ship

But I never wanted to be a spaceman.

Sometimes, it's like that;
you spend time looking up at midnight
And, right away, everyone thinks
that's where you want to be

Take love, for example.

Picture Walls

Someday I'll find a house
with a thousand rooms
and make it mine.
Someday I'll hang a wall
with all the pictures
locked in my mind.

Two Happys

And, at last, I asked a child,
What is Christmas?

He simply hugged himself and smiled.
It's the only day with two happys,
he said.

Happy I got when I get up.
Happy I gave when I go to bed.

Down to the Sea

If you ask advice from me
When you go down to the sea
I'd advise taking a boap
Unless, of course, you can floap

Questions

Do you want to be a big girl?
No.
Don't you want to be like mommy?
No.
Do you have to go potty?
No.
Won't you even try?
No.
Are your pants wet?
No answer.

PART FOUR

The poems and lyrics in *Other Voices* were written over a long
period of time, in a variety of places, beginning with my first
published poem, *Divestment of Youth*, which appeared in the
Jackson High School student newspaper in 1957. Some were
written when I lived in Chicago working as a copywriter, some
while I was in the U.S. Coast Guard stationed in Cape May,
New Jersey, and others in Australia, California and Florida. The
songs *For The First Time* and *Xanadu*, created for the Eric Porter
Productions animated feature film *Marco Polo Jr.* were written
in collaboration with two marvelous musicians, Jack Grimsley
and Julian Lee. Jack also wrote the music for the songs *Yesterday
When The World Was Warm* and *Popcorn for Breakfast*.

Other Voices

Divestment of Youth

Whenever I see a tragic play
Or read where death split friends
I fear the reaper comes
Not for me, but other ones

Depressing thoughts press in upon me
Taking warmth and leaving cold bare soul
Stripped prematurely of youth's high wall
I stand alone, looking into each dank hole

I cringe!

And I see how death robs fruit from tree
My limbs fall limp
Each scythe's arc cuts a piece of me

Memories

Are memories made only
From the good times
It may be
But then why do poets
Spend so many hours
In search of sad rhymes

The Promises Lost

I could preen for hours
On the promises I've kept
And the sleep I didn't miss
If it weren't for those nights
On which I never slept
And the lips I didn't kiss
In my blinded right

Someday

Someday
I'm going to find the man
I really am
I'm going to do what
I know I can
I'm going to walk the line
That's in my hand

And someday
I'm going to face the dawn
Without the rain
I'm going to feel the joy
And not the pain
I'm going to give some love
And not in vain

Someday
When the clouds
Have washed away
When the sun
Comes home to stay
I'll taste the wine
On life I'll dine

Someday

Mistakes

I don't know why
We're so surprised
When they happen
After all, it's just a
Miss you take

Jon

You come with thousands of thoughts
Beyond my outstretched arms
And I hold hidden as many
From your unasked questions
And so we will sink the past
Like galleons full of false gold
And instead, seek the treasure
of the ship, Tomorrow

Alabama

Once men were brave
They found an open heart
They saw their job, knew their part
And followed even to the grave

But now bowed are the brave
Shut tight the open heart
They see their job, yet acknowledge no part

I can't help it if black is bad
And white is right
Through prejudice they rave

The Country of Mankind

I can see a new flag blowing in the wind
In a new land where everyone is kin
I can see a fine new country of the mind
I can see the Country of Mankind

I can see yellow, black and white hand in hand
In a place that's everyone's homeland
I can see a day when we're all color blind
I can see the Country of Mankind

It's not a land we'll ever find on a map
It's not the dream of some dictator's pap
It's just the dying of a false boundary line
Just the tearing down of fear walls in our minds

I can see one nation covering all the world
Where east and west battle flags are furled
I can see the plate of peace where all will dine
I can see the Country of Mankind

I can hear a new Anthem's melody of hope
From a new choir that knows it has to cope
I can see the answers we'll all finally find
I can see the Country of Mankind

Happy With Who I Am

Emmett Kelly reading Shakespeare
And Richard Burton telling jokes
JFK writing novels
And Mailer counting votes

Why is it every clown
Wants to be an actor
Every rain drop a grain of sand
Instead of doing well
At what they can

Never Were So Many So Few

I walk the windy streets of Chicago
Just to feel the lake song blow
And now and then I stop
Step into a crowded shop

Coffee steam and smoke curl 'round me
In my solitary booth as I watch the show
From the lighted shadows I see
And then I know

The way that man laughs
The way those two say hello
The way they softly smile
When the other gives the gaff

It's then slowly that I leave
Seeking air enough to breathe
My heart is sick and blue
For never were so many so few

Darlyn Clementine

I always questioned
the mothers who couldn't spell
who gave us all those talking heads on TV News
with names like Sussan, Loranine, and Mizchel

Was it something added on
along with pancake and Maybelline
by young and hungry egos in make-up rooms
at backwater KNBCs outside of Abilene?

But now I'm not so sure
Maybe they deserved those standout names
They could be like a friend of mine
She can spell and has never been near Abilene
I call her Darlyn Clementine

Telling Tales

Like Noah
You call to us
The endless variety of man
Offering refuge
In an ark of hope
Against a flood of human sand

And so with the dawn
We go two by two
Climbing the heights of Ararat Gold
And once again
Man tells the endless tale
He has always told

The Songs Unsung

We may have left
A thousand thoughts unsaid
A thousand gentle virgins unwed
But there are so many mountains left to go
So many Summers to walk through
And winter nights left to snow
That all the songs unsung
Will just have to go the way
Of bridesmaids

Mark

A baseball kid
And natural-born angler
Always dressed-up as someone
With friends in his wake

A pole vaulter
And paintballer
Always trying something new
With another project to make

A videographer
And surfer
Always looking for a story to tell
With a camera ready for another take

And finally
A musician
With rhythm in his hands
A boy turned to man
With a mark to make

Yesterday When The World Was Warm

Are these the winter days
Of all we've ever known
Has the frozen wind blown away
All the seeds we've ever sown
Is yesterday our only home
Yesterday, when you and I were born
Yesterday, when the world was warm

And has this snow that falls
Where children used to play
Come to tell us we've lost them all
The dreams we dreamed in yesterday
Yesterday, when you and I were born
Yesterday, when the world was warm

Yesterday, when rainbows chased the rain
Yesterday, when all was not in vain
Yesterday, before we faced the storm
Yesterday, when the world was warm

Is it now time to say goodbye
And we were wrong
And like the morning mist fade away
With the echo of our song
To yesterday, forever gone
Yesterday, when you and I were born
Yesterday, when the world was warm

May We Remember

In this season of giving
And right jolly olde elves
May we remember
To stuff every stocking
With the best we can give:
Ourselves!

Popcorn for Breakfast

I like red roses
And rain
I like vanilla ice cream
And the funny faces Jack Frost
Paints on winter's window panes
I like the smell of sun tan lotion
And gasoline
I like a song so sad it makes me cry

And I like
Popcorn for breakfast
And cornflakes in bed
I like violets in empty wine bottles
And long earrings jangling next to my head
I like milk chocolates at midnight
And candles and lace
I like a man who says he cares for me
And longs to place his lips close to my face

But I don't like
No, I don't like
I don't like that nobody don't like
That I like
Popcorn for breakfast

And I don't like
No, I don't like
I don't like that nobody don't like
That I do care
For fancy earrings and my hair

And I don't like
No, I don't like
I don't like that nobody don't like
When midnight comes
It's full of chocolate cracker crumbs

I like popcorn for breakfast
And babies who cry
I like promises from would be worn lovers
And the fading sunlight before it dies
I like the ocean in winter
The country in spring
I like a man who says he cares for me
And longs to talk of all the gifts he'll bring

But I don't like
No, I don't like
I don't like that nobody don't like
That I like popcorn for breakfast

And I don't like
No, I don't like
I don't like that nobody don't care
That when I look for my man
Nobody's there

I Remember My Months By The Sea

The moon was always quiet
Its golden, shining beams
dashed themselves earthward in silent
streams of yellow, blue, and bronze
And as they dashed, they were lashed
by the whipping winter winds
of a stark snowless December

How well I remember
and will remember that stark December
It was the last month while I lived
by the sea, by the rolling, windy sea
And in that December only tides told time
and moons marched the minutes away

As the endless seas splashed against
that distant sand beaded shore, over and over
I waited and counted the days watching
the gulls chase the moon across dark nights
I waited in that December, in the cold wind with
the sea, the screeching gulls and the tumbling tides

And I was reminded, ever reminded
that soon thirty would be three times over
Soon December would stop its moon from marching
and quietly give up its prisoner
Then would I leave the sea, the rolling windy sea
And the gulls would test my soul
with their screeching nevermore

The waiting would be over
The tides, the moon, and the rolling, windy sea
would be left behind, and I would come home
Home to the one I left behind

Nine Eleven

Our world has changed
That much is true
But as it ever was
How is up to me
And you

For the First Time

I have walked
And yet I'm walking for the first time.
I have seen, still I'm seeing for the first time.
Though I have heard many sweet sounds around me,
Somehow I'm hearing them all for the first time
And all the days without you
Somehow they seem just like a dream
Now I'm awake for the first time
The first time in my life

I have laughed
Yet I'm laughing for the first time
My foolish heart now is beating for the first time
I may have held other hands here in mine
Somehow I'm feeling the touch for the first time
Love is more than a word,
It's all I've heard it could be
It's you and me
You and me

His Gift

Amid the hustle
To find those special gifts
On longer and longer shopping lists
I sometimes worry
That the only one we miss
Is the Child who was born
On this December day

Then on Christmas morning
I watch the smiles, the loving looks
As each gift is opened
And I know that Child will not go wanting
For his gift is in our giving

A Long Goodbye

You never think of it that way
But that's what they are
The things you do
The words you say
As you go about
Your life
Day by day

Xanadu

North by west of Scorpio, beyond the Bear
Through the bow of Sagittarius standing there
In the spinning wheel that Ezekiel drew for us on air
Awaits my star

In those turning signs of fate that fill the sky
One tiny twinkling star is there, winking in my eye
My burning light, the light of life
Whispers down to me, come fly your future waits.
There you are my star, calling from afar
Whispering, come to me from where you are
As above, so above
Where you go, must I go
What you know, I must know
As above
So below

North by West of Scorpio, beyond the bear
I will find my fated destiny waiting there,
In the spinning wheel that Ezekiel drew for us on air
Awaits my star
Awaits my star
Awaits my star

Someone From Back Home

Every year someone from back home asks
How can you enjoy Christmas in Florida
And every year we wonder what makes them ask

Mel Torme` didn't invent Christmas
Neither did Bing

It's not the cold outside
That lets you enjoy Christmas
It's the warmth inside

The Monster In The Hall

I'll always remember that giggle
From the bedroom
When I played the monster,
Growling and gruffing
In the hall

And now sometimes when I pass that way
I listen for a moment and remember
How to smile

The Sounds of
Lyrics of Life
in four-part harmony

**Enjoy your own CD of the original
recordings for the record album**
Warm Harbor and Other Places to Hide
*10 poems recorded by author Larry Pontius
with music personally selected by him.*
*Includes Warm Harbor, Lancelots & Guiniveres, The Lemonade Tree,
Ten Cents Worth of Philosophy, How Far Away Is Far Away,
The Boob Tube, The Cost of Growing Up, Dusty Mornings,
The Second Million Times, Man & Wife*

Order your copy now for only $8.95 plus shipping.
Email *lpontius@earthlink.net* for details.

Printed in the United States
32556LVS00002B/142-168